P9-CFT-863

Alligators

ALICE TWINE

PowerKiDS press

New York

Published in 2008 by The Rosen Publishing Group, Inc.
29 East 21st Street, New York, NY 10010

First Edition

Editor: Amelie von Zumbusch
Book Design: Julio Gil
Photo Researcher: Nicole Pristash

Photo Credits: Cover, pp. 1, 5, 7, 9, 11, 13, 17, 19, 21, 23, 24 (top left, top right, bottom left, bottom right) Shutterstock.com; p. 15 © Chris Johns/Getty Images.

Library of Congress Cataloging-in-Publication Data

Twine, Alice.
  Alligators / Alice Twine. — 1st ed.
      p. cm. — (Baby animals)
  Includes index.
  ISBN 978-1-4042-4146-6 (library binding)
  1. Alligators—Infancy—Juvenile literature. I. Title.
  QL666.C925T95 2008
  597.98'4—dc22
                                        2007019961

Manufactured in the United States of America

Contents

Baby Alligators 4

Where Do Alligators Live? 12

A Baby Alligator's Life 14

Words to Know 24

Index 24

Web Sites 24

Can you guess what this small animal is? It is a baby alligator!

Newborn alligators are only 6 to 8 inches (15–20 cm) long. However, adult alligators are often as long as 13 feet (4 m)!

Baby alligators have yellow **stripes** on their skin. They will lose these stripes as they grow up.

Alligators have a rounded **snout**. They have lots of sharp teeth. Alligators use their teeth to catch food.

Alligators live in watery places, such as rivers, lakes, and **wetlands**.

Mother alligators lay many eggs. After about two months, baby alligators break out of the eggs.

Alligator mothers watch over their babies. The mothers keep the babies safe from animals that might want to eat them.

Alligators swim quietly through the water to catch their food. Young alligators eat bugs, small fish, frogs, and mice.

As all alligators do, baby alligators like to lie around in the sun.

Adult alligators live alone, but young alligators stick together. They form groups, called **pods**.

Words to Know

pod

snout

stripes

wetlands

Index

F

food, 10, 18

S

sunlight, 20

T

teeth, 10

W

wetlands, 12

Web Sites

Due to the changing nature of Internet links, PowerKids Press has developed an online list of Web sites related to the subject of this book. This site is updated regularly. Please use this link to access the list: www.powerkidslinks.com/baby/all/